I062091D

First published in the UK by HarperCollins Children's Books in 2008
1 3 5 7 9 10 8 6 4 2
ISBN 13 978-0-00-727835-0
ISBN 0-00-727835-7
A CIP catalogue record for this title is available from the British Library.

No part of this publication may be reproduced, stored in a retrieval system or transmitted
in any form or by any means, electronic, mechanical, photocopying, recording
or otherwise, without the prior permission of HarperCollins Publishers Ltd,
77-85 Fulham Palace Road, Hammersmith, London W6 8JB.
www.harpercollinschildrensbooks.co.uk
All rights reserved

Basil Brush ®:© 2008 Ivan Owen's Estate and Peter Firmin
under exclusive licence to Entertainment Rights Plc. All rights reserved.
Basil's Angels is based on a story by Ben Ward

Printed and bound in Italy by Rotolito Lombarda SpA

ANNUAL 2009

HarperCollins *Children's Books*

Welcome!

This Basil Brush Annual belongs to:

. . . .

Age:

. . . .

For one
night only,

. . . .

will be the **star**
of the show!

Contents

Join the Stars!

Check out our mini fact file cards! There's a space for you to make your own fact card, too. Write down four mini facts about yourself, pop in a silly photograph and join our spankingly outrageous show! He he!

* Basil Brush *

Loves: jelly babies and being famous
Hates: not getting enough sleep
Hobby: change
Beauty fact: he has his own stylist

* Anil *

Favourite saying: innit
Past: kept his niece, Lucy, as a slave!
Hobby: making rotten food
Secret fact: he used to be a dinner lady

* Madison *

Favourite saying: Bay-zill!
Loves: clothes, shoes, bags, singing
Ambition: to design dresses
Star fact: rescued Lucy from life as a slave

★ Dave ★

Favourite outfit:
designer suit, bought on a deal
Secret fact: he's a real softie!
Favourite smell: money!
Favourite toy: calculator

★ Liam ★

Motto: try, fail. Try again, fail better!
Likes: the lay-deeez!
Embarrassing moment:
dressing up as a chicken

★ You! ★

Fact 1: . . . .
Fact 2: . . . .
Fact 3: . . . .
Fact 4: . . . .

★ Lucy ★

Family: Anil's niece
Loves: her friends
Hates: Cousin Mortimer's tricks
Embarrassing moment:
falling over in a dance competition!

★ Mortimer ★

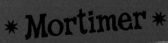

Loves: cheating, sneaking
and parties
Hates: coppers
Hobby: avoiding prison
Middle name: Trouble

Quiz that Fox!

Want to hear my deepest, darkest secrets? Then delve into this foxy interview and learn everything you need to know, and everything you don't need to know, about moi! Go easy on me now!

What was your early life like?
Chris P Bacon, age 10

A lot of people think I am rather posh but no, us Brushes were as poor as old church mice. When the wolf was at our door he brought his own sandwiches! He he! And my poor old mother couldn't afford posh talcum powder so she used self-raising flour on me. Whenever I got hot I would break out in pancakes! **BOOM! BOOM!**

How long have you been saying your catchphrase 'Boom! Boom!'?
Pea Body, age 7

Well, I wouldn't exactly call it a catchphrase. More of a warcry or a polished proverb. People for centuries to come will be hailing 'Boom! Boom!'. Even when the robots have taken over, my 'Boom! Boom!' will be heard across the galaxy! Maybe they'll change it to 'Zoom! Zoom!'.

But seriously, it's a great family tradition. My old ancestor, Sir Lancelot de Brush used to say 'Ye Boom! Ye Boom!'. It's been in the family for hundreds of years – a bit like some of my jokes!

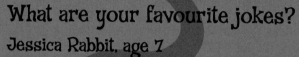

What are your favourite jokes?
Jessica Rabbit, age 7

Well then, Jessica Rabbit, that's a hard one. Being such a giggle wizard, where do I begin? He he! I think one of my favourites must be the one about the pig who left the pigsty because the others were taking him for grunted. **BOOM! BOOM!** Oh and I couldn't leave out the one about the Dutch girl with inflatable shoes. I was going to ask her out on a date, but she popped her clogs! But my favourite one of the day is this beauty: What do Mexicans have under their carpets? Underlay! Underlay! **BOOM! BOOM!** Come on, you'd have to pull a lot of crackers to find quality gags like that!

How old are you?

Lou Zar, age 8

Ah ha! That would be telling. A fox never discloses such secrets. Still young enough to be a hit with the lay-deez! I'll have you know I've still got all my own teeth – in a glass by my bed! **He he! BOOM! BOOM**

What's your favourite food?

Marsha Mellow, age 6

I love jelly babies! I adore them with a passion that verges on the indecent. I have eaten them since I was a little cub and could easily eat my whole body weight in jelly babies. You should see my jelly belly!

Have you got a girlfriend?

Dan Druff, age 8

I have a vixen in every port, just waiting for the day they might get to see this showbiz fox again. He he! Seriously though, I don't have a girlfriend at the moment. I was engaged for quite a long time, but people kept banging on the cubicle door saying they needed the loo! Oh, come on, show some respect for the elderly!

Did you like school?

Joe Kerr, age 9

Well, I was a bit of a joker at school. But I was also the teacher's pet. They used to keep me in a cage in the staff room! **He he!**

Now that's enough Brushy secrets for now, my cheeky fans! This foxy interview will continue later, on page 40...

Mortimer's Wordsearch

Nothing like a cheeky little puzzle to pull at your floppy brain strings. Cousin Mortimer has made this sneaky wordsearch, filled with all of his favourite words. The words can read up, down, backwards or diagonally. Have fun in Mortimer's world of darkness…

Criminal
Trickery
Secrets
Escape
Sewers
Hide
Naughty
Steal
Tomfoolery
Jokes
Bang Bang
Lies
Fool

R	E	T	Y	O	I	P	L	E	F	C	I	T	T	O	P	O	A
E	U	F	S	H	D	E	R	T	Y	I	O	P	S	L	E	D	S
S	L	A	N	I	M	I	R	C	T	G	M	R	T	R	P	O	D
D	H	G	F	D	F	N	R	R	Z	S	E	W	E	R	S	H	R
F	S	H	K	T	R	T	A	O	P	N	N	D	A	D	O	T	T
R	E	B	N	R	T	I	O	U	O	T	P	I	L	F	Y	O	C
B	D	A	C	E	F	R	D	N	G	H	U	R	E	O	T	M	U
N	N	N	S	E	R	T	I	D	I	H	Y	T	V	O	R	F	I
O	I	T	D	P	S	S	E	C	R	E	T	S	U	L	E	R	J
O	L	H	I	D	E	A	T	E	K	H	L	Y	T	S	S	E	K
W	P	E	P	O	Y	T	E	R	N	E	N	C	P	C	C	L	R
A	J	N	R	S	A	R	T	E	D	C	R	N	O	V	D	Y	T
S	T	O	M	F	O	O	L	E	R	Y	F	Y	L	I	E	S	Y
C	O	T	K	I	C	T	P	T	H	L	I	P	T	Y	P	I	S
N	I	E	Y	E	T	R	I	N	C	K	B	L	R	U	O	U	T
B	T	R	O	D	S	E	R	E	P	A	C	S	E	I	L	Y	R
K	G	F	W	E	R	D	S	E	F	L	K	J	H	L	K	G	E
E	W	E	R	T	B	A	N	G	B	A	N	G	H	C	A	S

Jigsaw Jangles

Check out this party popping photo! Prove your intelligence and see if you can find where the missing pieces go. Don't say I don't give you fascinating and mind bending tasks, my loyal lovers! He he!

1.
5.
2.
6.
3.
7.
4.
8.

Now turn over for a whiz-popping photo story from one my favourite episodes from our TV show – Basil's Angels. Comin' atcha, foxbusters!

Basil's Angels

Let's start by setting the scene, my worthy book worms. The show begins with Anil and Madison setting up a magic night...

"A magic evening is a great idea, Anil!" Madison screeched. "It sounds totally awesome!"

"It better be. My wand cost one pound fifty! That's more than my car is worth!" Anil said, as he took an old toy car out of his pocket.

"What wand?" Madison asked, as Anil pulled a toilet roll out of his pocket.

"That's not a wand!" Madison screeched. "It's an old toilet roll – eww!"

"It belonged to an old hypnotist I knew," Anil began.

"You have some strange friends, Anil," Liam said, shaking his head.

→ Enter Basil

"Why is Anil holding an old toilet roll up in the air?" Basil asked. "Surely that is cruelty against toilet rolls. It just wants to get to the bottom! **BOOM! BOOM!**"

"It's his wand," Madison whispered. "For the magic night."

"Oh no! I can't stand magic, especially that disappearing act Dave does every time the bill arrives. Ha ha!" Basil chuckled.

"Well, I think it's going to be great!" Madison replied.

"Maybe the wand will turn Anil's sandwiches into something completely different… like **FOOD!**" twittered Basil.

"There's nothing wrong with my food, innit," Anil replied, as he shoved a piece of smelly mush into his mouth.
He then burst into a fit of coughing and spat the food out in a gooey lump!
"Ok, ok, so I could have added a bit more salt."

"Anil, you're so gross!" Madison grimaced, as she dodged out of the way of Anil's flying food. "Now, it's time for the magic show of the year! Anil, please step forward for our first trick!"
Anil stepped up into a box and Madison closed the door. When she opened the door again, Anil was gone! Everyone cheered and clapped when they saw that Anil had disappeared.
"And now by the power of the magic, er, toilet roll… behold! He returns!" she yelped, as she flung open the door.
As the door opened again, Anil was standing back in the box. This time, the act didn't receive a rapturous applause. In fact, it received no applause whatsoever.
"Charming," Anil muttered.

Anil began the next trick.

"Dave has let me use this super expensive ruby, innit," Anil said, as everyone stared at the shiny ruby. "It's, like, worth more than the king of Emerald City and all his emerald children and their emerald pets."

"Hey, be careful!" Dave shouted, as Anil pretended to eat the ruby. "I'm being paid to look after it for the Museum of Very Expensive Jewels and Even More Expensive Chef's Skulls."

"Now, Bay-zill – I think you should go next!" Madison said, as she dragged Basil up to the stage.

"Magic is for losers," Basil grumbled. "No-one can trick a fox like me!"

Madison reached into Basil's pocket and started to pull out a string of flags from his pocket.

"Hold on, I think this one is stuck," Madison said, smiling.

As she tugged on the flags, a pair of purple flowery boxer shorts flew out of the end!

"What the Dickens?" giggled Basil, as he covered himself up. "Crikey - I thought it was a bit draughty up there! He he!"

"Basil lost his boxer shorts!" Anil cried, as he rolled about the floor in tears of laughter.

✳

"Alright, alright," Basil smirked. "Please – let a fox keep his dignity!" Just then, Dave let out a shriek.

"The ruby!" he cried. "It's gone!"

Cue dramatic drum noise that is often used in these situations!

DUM DUM DUUUUUM!

"Nobody can leave until we have found the ruby," Madison said, calmy.

"I can feed everyone, innit," Anil said.

"We'll arrest you if you try it," joked Liam.

"He got three years for a pork pie once!" Basil giggled.

"You better stop joking, there's a detective over there," Liam said, as he pointed to a man in a trench coat.

The detective began questioning everyone.

"Everyone empty their pockets," the detective said. "A serious crime has been committed."

"I haven't got it," Basil said. "Go on, search me. Go easy around the ribs. I'm ticklish!"

The detective put his hand in Basil's pocket and there was the magic ruby!

"Basil!" everybody shouted.

"I didn't do it!" Basil shouted. "I must have been framed!"

"I'm very disappointed in you, Basil," Liam said, shaking his head.

"But, but… I didn't steal it!" Basil replied, astonished.

Madison looked to the floor, embarrassed.

"Bay-zill, he found it in your pocket," she said, quietly.

"Basil Brush, I am arresting you for theft. You are going to prison for a long time," the detective said. "Don't make this difficult for yourself. Come with me."

"But I didn't do it," Basil said, fiercely.

Suddenly, Basil ducked underneath the detective and sped out of the door!

The detective grabbed his walkie-talkie.

"We've got a fox on the run!"

Over at Crime Botch studio, Jessica Lovely was reporting on the missing thief. "On today's programme viewers are warned to look out for this international jewel thief," Jessica Lovely reported to the world. "He is thought to be armed with some extremely dangerous jokes!"

Meanwhile, over at Basil's flat, Madison and Lucy were watching the TV report about Basil.

"I don't believe he did it!" said Lucy, sadly.

"I agree with you!" replied Madison. "He's totally innocent."

"I miss Basil," Lucy sighed.

"I remember when he once organised us into a team called 'Basil's Angels'. Whenever he needed us the red box would start flashing!" Madison laughed.

Just then, the red box started flashing and Basil's head suddenly appeared!

"Good evening, angels," Basil said, through the red box.

Madison lifted up the red box and Basil popped out. "To be honest, I don't know why we bother with the box," Madison said as she rolled her eyes.

"Madison, I need your help!" cried Basil. "I need the angels to investigate who set me up!"

"But I'm the only angel left," Madison replied.

"We'll need another angel then," Basil began. "But who can we ask?"

Lucy started jumping up and down, waving her hands in the air.

"Lucy, can you think of anyone?" Basil grinned, as Lucy screamed in frustration. "Only joking! You can be in the team."

"And I know who would make a perfect third," Madison said.

On cue, Liam sauntered into the flat. Basil had his three angels! The Basil's Angels had been formed. Now all they had to do was find a good disguise.

"Ah, once upon a time, there were three lovely girls…" Basil began before being loudly interrupted by Liam coughing. "I'm sorry, two lovely girls and one lovely *boy*…"
"That's better!" Liam frowned.

✶

Suddenly, Liam, Lucy and Madison transformed into Basil's Angels! They were dressed in black leather cat suits and Liam was wearing a peroxide blonde wig!

"Now they work for me," Basil said, in a booming voice. **"My name is Baaaaaasssssssiiiiiiiiiiiiiii!"**

✶

"I look like an idiot!" Liam groaned, fiddling with his wig.

"If you're worried about that, you're in the wrong show!" Lucy giggled. "Don't worry, Liam. You'll get used to it," Madison said, hiding her laughter. "Come on Angels, let's go to work!"

Meanwhile, Basil went into hiding. But everywhere he went, WANTED posters with his face on were posted onto the walls.

✶

"Maybe I'll be safe in this alleyway, they'll never find me here," Basil said when suddenly a spotlight hit the wall right next to him!

Basil froze to the spot.
"This fugitive business
isn't easy," he panted.
"But at least I can
count on my friends."
Just then, Basil
spotted Dave.

"How much is the reward for the
capture of Basil Brush? Is that cash?"
Dave whispered into his phone.
"Most of them anyway! Tut-tut-tut!"
Basil frowned.

A loud clanking noise was coming from
a bin next to Basil. Suddenly Cousin
Mortimer sprang out of the bin!
"Will you keep the bloomin' noise down!"
Mortimer said, wiping the rubbish off
his clothes. "Some people are trying
to sleep!"
"Mortimer! I need your help! I'm a
fugitive. I've got to hide out for a few
days," Basil said, quickly.
"In that case, Baz, step into my office,"

Mortimer replied, opening the bin lid further.
"I'm not getting in a dustbin!" Basil cried,
horrified. "I'm a dashing young fox, don't
you know?"

"This ain't no ordinary dustbin," Mortimer
chuckled, as he opened the door. Floods
of laughter and cork-popping streamed
out of the bin. "It's the party bin!"
"Your secret hideout is in the sewers?!"
Basil exclaimed. "But what about
the smell?"
"Yeah, you do pong a bit, but don't
worry, the others'll get used to you!
Bang! Bang!"

Meanwhile, the angels were hard at work.
Madison was fobbing off the detective
dressed in a mime costume.
Lucy was looking for clues dressed
as a business man.
But Liam was still having problems.
He was now dressed as a *chicken*

Suddenly, Basil burst through the trapdoor
and gave Liam a fright.
"Basil! Where did you come from?"
he asked.
"Mortimer's sewers. It's amazing!
You should have a look," Basil replied.
"I'm not going in the sewers!" Liam replied.
"Why? Are you a **CHICKEN?**" Mortimer
chuckled. **"Bang! Bang!"**

Basil's Angels were still trying to work out
who could have stolen the missing ruby.
"Apart from us lot, the only person who
went anywhere near the stage was Anil,"
Liam said.
"Anil's not a thief. A poisoner maybe,
but not a thief. He he!" chuckled Basil.
"Maybe Anil's toilet roll stole it!"
"Mmmm. We don't know much about
where he got that from other than
it was from an old hypnotist friend,"
thought Madison.
Then Madison suddenly jumped up into
the air. "I know what happened!"
"Well, aren't you going to tell us?" asked
Liam, excitedly.
"Of course she isn't. This is a story, she's
going to save it up for the big ending!
He he!" Basil giggled.
The Angels put a plan into action.

They tipped off the detective that Basil may be in the café and Mortimer set about dressing up Basil so he could slip into the café unnoticed.

When everything was ready, Mortimer unveiled the new Basil.

"Introducing, my distant cousin, sister Basilica Brush!" Mortimer announced to the café, as Basil hobbled in behind him dressed as a **NUN!**

"They are not going to fall for this!" Basil

whispered to Mortimer, adjusting his holy hood.

"It'll be fine. So long as nobody gives the game away," Mortimer replied.

Suddenly Dave marched up to Basilica and Mortimer and started pointing and shouting. "Officer. That is Basil Brush!

Now I would like to collect my reward!"

"Thanks for your support, Dave," muttered Basil, under his breath.

"Don't be ridiculous. You should have more respect for a woman of the cloth," the detective said. "I'm sorry about him Sister Basilica."

"Yes, you're not the only one," Basil replied in a squeaky voice.

Basil looked around and wondered where Madison was. "She should have been here by now," Basil tutted. "She's always late."

"Yes, that's a nasty **HABIT,**" Mortimer chuckled. **"Bang! Bang!"**

"And just in case you're worrying that there may be more jokes like that, dear reader, be rest assured – there are nun. **Boom! Boom!"**

→ Enter Madison dressed as a newsreader

"Tonight we are recording a reconstruction of the ruby being stolen!" Madison said, in her best newsreading voice.

"I can play the part of this naughty Basil Brush," Basil squeaked, and then turned to Mortimer. "I hope no-one realises it's really me."

Dave placed the ruby on the cushion and everyone got into place. As Anil pulled the flags out of Basil's pocket, out popped his boxer shorts again!

"I believe these are your boxer shorts, Sister Basilica!" Anil shouted, waving the toilet roll in the air. Suddenly, the ruby appeared in Basil's hands!

"You are Basil Brush! I'm arresting you for theft – again!" the detective shouted. "And for the unlawful disguise of a lady of the cloth!"

"But I didn't do it!" Basil cried, as he looked around for help.

"Bad luck, cuz. I'll tell you what, why don't I take the ruby for safekeeping?" Mortimer said, then nodded at Madison. "I might take the brunette too, while I'm at it!"

Suddenly Madison stepped forward into the chaos.

"No, it proves he **isn't** the thief," she said.

"Why don't you leave the crime solving to us!" the detective snapped. "You're just a TV crew."

"Actually, we're not just a TV crew. We're…"

DAH-DAH-DAH! Basil's Angels!

"Here's what happened," Madison began. "Basil did take the ruby, but he was hypnotised into doing it."

"Hypnotised?" Anil asked.

"The hypnotist gave Basil a trigger phrase," Madison said, as everyone gasped. "Whenever he hears a certain word he steals something! Anil used the phrase in his act, and when Basil heard it, he stole the ruby!"

Madison shouted the words **'BOXER SHORTS'** and suddenly Basil was holding Dave's wallet.

"Are you going to nick something everytime one of us says **'BOXER SHORTS'?"** Dave asked.

Suddenly Basil was holding a watch.

"Hey!" Anil shouted. "That's my watch, innit!"

"But who could have hypnotised me?" Basil asked.

"This is what took me a while to figure out," Madison began. "The clue lies in this toilet roll!"

"Hey, that's my wand, innit!" Anil replied.

"But where did you get it from?" Madison asked.

"From an old hypnotist friend I once knew, back in the day," Anil started.

"Exactly!" Madison said. "Your hypnotist friend must have hypnotised you to hypnotise others whenever you use this toilet roll!"

"I think you might be right," Anil said scratching his head. "The last time I used this toilet roll, a man named One Eyed Jack stole a glass eye from a granny. He got 3 years."

"I've got to admit. I didn't see that coming," Mortimer chuckled.

"There's only one thing to do with this wand now, then," Anil said as he walked over to the toilet and flushed it down the pan. "Sorry, Basil."

"I'm a free fox without a stain on my reputation!" Basil cried, happily. "The whole world knows that I am not a thief!"

"I'm totally proud of you, Basil," said Madison.

"Thank you, everyone!" Basil replied, happily. "Now you'll have to excuse me. I've got to put this outfit back before the nuns realise I nicked it! He he! **BOOM! BOOM!"**

THE END

Memory Game

Phew! That was a close one. It could have been curtains for me. A convict in fox fur was cunningly averted! I don't think prison overalls would suit my silky brush, somehow! Now did you pay attention, Brushingtons? It's time to take Lucy's super quiz to find out just how much you remember about Basil's Angels.

No peeking 'til you've answered everything!

1.
What was the name of the programme that Jessica Lovely was reporting on?

2.
Who was going to hand Basil to the police for a reward?

3.
What did Basil appear in when Lucy and Madison were watching TV?

4.
What was happening inside Mortimer's bin?

5.
Where did Basil find Cousin Mortimer?

6.
Who discovered the true thief?

7.
What were the secret words that hypnotised Basil?

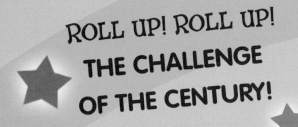

ROLL UP! ROLL UP! THE CHALLENGE OF THE CENTURY!

Reader Vs Fox

Check out this crazy list of factual mayhem! Can you challenge this cunning fox and find out which statements are true and which ones are false? I've written my own answers next to each one. Once you have written your own answers down, check the answers on page 60 and add up both of our scores.

1. A crocodile's tongue is attached to the roof of its mouth

Basil: **False**   You: . . . .

2. The fox is the most intelligent and beautiful animal in the kingdom

Basil: **True**   You: . . . .

3. The average person eats eight spiders in their sleep in their lifetime

Basil: **True**   You: . . . .

4. Spider webs were used to cure warts during the Middle Ages

Basil: **True**   You: . . . .

5. The wind only ever blows south in the Sahara Desert

Basil: **False**   You: . . . .

6. People born in Alaska have blue tongues

Basil: **True**   You: . . . .

7. The ancient dinosaur, Polygranthus, had eight legs

Basil: **True**   You: . . . .

8. A kangaroo is the size of a bee when it is first born

Basil: **False**   You: . . . .

The winner is:

. . . .

Boom! Boom!

Some **booming** jokes to tickle your tonsils!

A boy went to a Halloween party with a sheet on his head. "Are you a ghost?" asked his friends

★

"No, I'm an unmade bed!"

What did the monkey say when it got into a hot bath?

★

Oooh-oooh-oooh-aaah-aaah-aaah!

Why are chefs hard to like?

★

Because they beat eggs, whip cream and mash potatoes!

Why did the sea turn?

★

Because the sea-weed!

Why did the bald man paint rabbits on his head?

★

Because from a distance they looked like hares

What do you call
a chicken that's been
run over by a truck?
★
Coq au Van

What do you
call a pig with
three eyes?
★
Piiig

Why don't owls
go on dates
when it rains?
★
**Because it's too
wet to woo**

Why did the
spaceship land outside
the bedroom?
★
**Because someone
left the landing
light on**

Who are the moodiest
animals in the zoo?
★
**Camels – they've always
got the hump**

Anil's Food Challenge

Spoons at the ready, bowls at your service, gunge on the walls. . . Do you dare take part in Anil's cook-a-thon? Will it be toxic? Will it smell like frogs' eggs? Will you puke in the toilet? There's only one way to find out, my brave fox lovers. Go forth and pick up that saucy spoon!

ANIL'S RECIPES OF DEATH

Dead Man's Claw
. . . .

You will need:
* 1 clear latex glove
* Red or orange fruit juice
* Bowl full of punch

Directions:
1. Clean the latex glove before use
2. Fill the glove up with colourful juice
3. Put an elastic band around the filled glove
4. Place carefully in the freezer
5. When frozen, peel off the glove leaving the formed ice hand
6. Put the ice hands in a bowl of punch and watch the severed hand float! A perfect trick to shock your family! He he!

Gooey Earwax Trick

You will need:
* Mini marshmallows
* Peanut butter
* Cotton buds

Directions:

1. Break off the cotton parts of the buds and throw the cotton away

2. Place a mini marshmallow on each end of the stick

3. Dip or spread mini marshmallows with peanut butter and set out on a plate with some normal cotton buds to really trick people!

Euh! Wait 'til you see how gross this looks!!

A Riddle for a Reader

See if you can solve this lot of tantalising brain teasers. Don't be fooled – they might not be quite as they seem...

★

If a plane crashed on the border of England and Scotland, where would they bury the survivors?

★

If there's a frog, dead in the centre of a lilypad which is right in the middle of the pond, which side would it jump to?

★

A man went outside in the pouring rain with no protection, but not a hair on his head got wet... how come?

★

If the red house is on the right side and if the blue house is on the left side where's the white house?

★

What grows bigger the more you take out of it?

Boom to the Maximus

We've all come up with our favourite jokes du jour. Impress your friends with this load of cackle inducers. Pop your funniest joke in the space in the middle and see which one gets the biggest giggle!

What do crabs wear?

★

Shell suits!

What's brown and smelly and sounds like a church bell?

★

Dung!

What do you call a French man in sandals?

★

Philippe Floppe!

Where do policemen live?

★

999 Letsby Avenue

What did one fish say to the other fish?

★

I've haddock up to here with you!

Insert your own giggling gumbo here

What did the beaver say when it swam into a wall?

★

Dam!

Why are football pitches always wet?

★

Because the players dribble so much!

Welcome to
the Basil Brush
Journey of Laughter

You will need:

✳ A fellow foxy friend

✳ A dice

✳ Some tonsil tickling jokes

Aim of the game:

First one to reach me is the winner!

If you land on Anil, you must go back

to the beginning!

Good luck!

START	2
11	12
21	Uh oh! Anil gives you a bad case of the windy pops **Go back 2 places to recover.**
31	32
41	42
51	52
61	62
71	72
Who can shout 'Boom! Boom!' **the loudest? The winner goes forward 8 places.**	82
91	92

3	4	5	You lose Basil's super styling mousse. **Go back one place.**	7	8	9	10

| Tell five jokes in 60 seconds! **Go back to the start if you fail.** | 14 | 15 | 16 | You help Mortimer hide in the sewers. **Go forward 3 places.** | 18 | 19 | 20 |

| 23 | 24 | | 26 | 27 | 28 | Along with Dave, you have been caught selling out of date prunes. **Go back 3 places.** | 30 |

| Tell a joke about school. **Go forward 2 places if you make your opponent laugh.** | 34 | 35 | 36 | Basil beats you at karaoke. **Go back 3 places.** | 38 | | 40 |

| You give Basil 20 red jelly babies! **Go forward 3 places.** | 44 | 45 | 46 | You rescue Madison from Mortimer's terrible jokes! **Go forth 4 places.** | 48 | 49 | Mortimer has a challenge for you. **Tell a joke about animals in the next 10 seconds or go back 10 places!** |

| 53 | Tell two 'knock knock' jokes in 30 seconds. **Jump forward 4 places if you succeed.** | 55 | 56 | 57 | 58 | You forget to tell Liam that his date cancelled. **Go back 2 places.** | 60 |

| 63 | 64 | You accidentally eat some of Anil's rotten egg gravy. **Go back 3 places.** | 66 | 67 | 68 | Congratulations! You win a place on The Basil Brush Show. **Go forward 8 places!** | 70 |

| 73 | 74 | 75 | Tell your opponent a naughty joke! **Go forward 4 places if you make them laugh.** | 77 | 78 | 79 | 80 |

| 83 | | 85 | 86 | 87 | 88 | 89 | 90 |

| 93 | 94 | 95 | 96 | 97 | 98 | 99 | **FINISH!** Congratulations! You are the funniest fox on the planet! |

The Shrinking Dave

Pay attention, you ferocious fox lovers! Our Dave is in need of some serious help. He dabbled in some strange magic dust and now he is the size of a turnip!

Speaking of turnips, have I ever told you about my old schoolmaster who once gave me a terrible telling off? He said, "Basil, you never turnip for maths, you never turnip for english, in fact you rarely turnip for anything!" **BOOM! BOOM!** That was one from the old jokes home!

Right, now where was I?

Guide Dave through this mega maze, collecting the mini tomatoes on the way. Try and collect as many tomatoes as you can – they are the only thing that can ping him back to Man-Size-Dave. If you run into Mortimer, you must start again! If you do fail, however, we can always put Dave on the mantelpiece and charge people from around the world to come and see a real life 'Turnip-Man'. Think of all the money! He he! Ahem – now on with the game. **Good luck, my bezzies!**

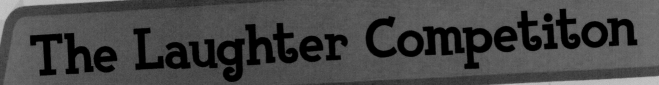

The Laughter Competiton

So my mini giggle wizards – you think you are funnier than me, do you? After launching a wicked joke competition, I think some of you may pip me to the funny post! After stomping through a gigantic amount of joketastic entries from my foxy fans - we have decided that these beauties are the winners! So congratulations – you are officially my funniest fans **EVER!** Don't go stealing my day job though!

What do you get if you cross a toad with a science fiction film?
Star Warts!

✸ Ianna Reeve ✸

Why did Granny put wheels on her rocking chair?
Because she wanted to Rock n' Roll

✸ Daniel Alexander ✸

What did the biscuit say when he got run over?
Oh crumbs!

✸ Emma Driver ✸

What do you call two robbers?
A pair of knickers!

✸ Alaska-lilly Rachael Gadd ✸

Who are the moodiest animals in the zoo?
Camels – they've always got the hump!

✸ Matthew Cayombe ✸

What do you call a cow eating grass?
A lawn-mooer!

✸ Alice Parker ✸

What do you call a pig studying karate?
A pork chop

✸ Daniel Partridge ✸

How many donkeys can you fit on a fire engine?
One on the right, one on the left, and one on the top saying 'eeoh eeoh'!

✸ Qianyun Liang ✸

A man walks into a pub and says,
"Do you have any helicopter flavour crisps?"
"No, Sir," the barman replies.
"We only have PLANE!"

✳ Rowan Nunn ✳

Why did the golfer wear
two pairs of trousers?
In case he got a hole in one!

✳ Nathan Lauren ✳

"Sir Sir, my pen's run out!"
"Run after it then!"

✳ Andrew Williamson ✳

What do you call a wizard with a cold?
Harry Snotter

✳ Tayne Campbell ✳

One cow said to the other cow,
"About this mad cow disease,
it's a bit worrying, isn't it?"
The other cow said, "I'm not
worried at all, I'm a duck!"

✳ Kitty Riley ✳

What is yellow and dangerous?
Shark infested custard!

✳ Emma Marshall ✳

What do pirates say when they're cold?
Shiver-me-timbers!

✳ Rory Afrizal ✳

Why do fish live in salt water?
Because pepper makes them sneeze!

✳ Ghada Kassab ✳

How do you fix a broken chimpanzee?
With a monkey wrench!

✳ Stella Gibson ✳

What do you get if you cross
a cow and a stereo?
A moooooooosical!

✳ Sophie Bratherton ✳

What do you get if you cross
bubblebath with a famous detective?
Sherlock Foams!

✳ Oliver Booth ✳

Quiz that Fox - part deux

Here we go again! Be kind to me!

Who do you think is the better looking fox - you or Mortimer?

Teresa Green, age 8 1/2

I beg your pudding?! Little Miss Green Trees, there is surely only one answer to that question. Did I not mention that I came first in a beauty contest? Ok, ok, so the only other contestant was a skeleton and they disqualified him because he was a no body but it still counts! Boom! Boom!

What is your favourite costume?

Norman Pooman, age 7

Well, I have to say Master Pooman, anything to do with spooky costumes are my favourite. I dressed up as a vampire once and I got so many compliments, I spent the whole evening saying, 'fangs very much, fang you'! He he! Oh, it's the way I tell 'em!

Is it hard work being a showbiz fox?

Penny Lane, age 9

Well, if it wasn't for my slave-like attitude, my unquestionable thirst for success and my roaring ambition, along with a whole team of lowly slaves, minions and yes-men to pander to my every desire, then I would say it's a piece of jelly baby cake! He he! Only joking. I wish!

What's your secret to looking young?

Nicho Lass, age 10

Why, thank you! You are my number one fan! Well, I do work out everyday. I work out what I'm going to scran for breakfast, lunch and dinner! **Boom! Boom!**

How have you remained so fashionable throughout your years as a showbiz fox?

Robin Banks, age 6

I have a personal stylist. And the things she says are very personal indeed. He he! Your mum and dad might remember me from the seventies when I was wearing flares. The trouble with wearing flares is that I kept on attracting rescue teams! **Boom! Boom!**

£1.20
1-7 September 2008

THE DAILY BRUSH

SHOCK DANCE PLOT REVEALED!

A PLOT TO SABOTAGE a major dance competition was uncovered yesterday. The dancers are said to be in shock after finding a tub of oil, ten banana skins and some steel marbles under a competitor's costume.

Mortimer Brush, fellow star of The Basil Brush Show, was found with the incriminating objects. He denies all charges.

Lucy and Liam, a dancing team, were appalled at the discovery. "We couldn't understand why we kept slipping over," Lucy said, shocked. "We couldn't even do our five point star twirly twizzle," recalled Liam, sadly.

Mortimer had covered the dance floor with oil and banana skins, causing some serious clumsy action. Mortimer insists the materials were for him. "The oil is to tame my furry ears, the marbles are for luck and the bananas are for my good health," Mortimer added. Upon being asked why he had ten banana skins, he grinned: "Because they like to hang around in bunches. Bang! Bang!" The stars are deciding whether to press charges. **THE CASE CONTINUES.**

HAVE YOU SEEN THESE PEOPLE?

BEWARE – Do NOT approach them! They are armed with terrible jokes and could cause fatal laughter.

BASIL BRUSH
IN KING PRAWN DRAMA

YESTERDAY Basil Brush was left reeling after a mystery person planted a smelly trick on him. At 5pm on Tuesday evening, Basil noticed a slightly fishy smell coming from his dressing room. Ever the professional, he used a peg to block his snout and carried on as normal.

But after a group of fans noticed the strange smell and posted it on Basil's blog, he realised he must act upon this strange crime.

After hours of sniffing, it was soon revealed that somebody had hidden one trout, two dirty socks and a king prawn behind his mirror.

Basil is appealing for any information and had this message for the culprit: "If they wanted some of my money, I could have told them to go to the prawn broker! Boom! Boom!"

He is appealing to anyone with a fishy aroma.

ANIL'S CAFÉ

THE BEST PLACE IN TOWN TO GET GROSS FOOD FROM A CRAZY COOK!

WINNER

OF THE WORST GRAVY AWARD 2007

HONOURARY MEMBER OF POISONOUS FOODS UNITED

DAILY SPECIALS:

SMELLY CHEESE SANDWICHES
MOULDY MINCED WORM PASTRIES
CREAMED BOGIE PIE
ROTTEN LIVER MILKSHAKES
COME AND TRY FOR YOURSELF!

✴ **ROOMMATE WANTED!** ✴
MUST LOVE DIRTY DRIPPING WALLS, POO SMELLS AND THE OCCASIONAL RAT. PARTIES PROMISED EVERY NIGHT AND NAUGHTY JOKERS PREFERRED. STRICTLY NO POLICE ALLOWED. CONTACT **MASTER M BRUSH** AT THE SEWERS, SEWERVILLE, SEWER TOWN ✴✴✴✴✴

JOKES CORNER

Why did the hedgehog cross the road?
To visit its flat mate!

✴

What do sheep do on sunny days?
Have a baa - baa - cue!

✴

What do you call a vampire that lives in the kitchen?
Spatula!

Spot the Difference

Intergalactic Brush at your service!
I do hope I remembered to pack my launch box.
Boom! Boom! He he! Can you spot
five differences between these planetary pics?

What do you do when you see a spaceman?
★
Park in it, man!

Stitch Me Up, Maddy!

1. **2.** **3.** **4.**

Madison has been working on some funky new patterns for her oh-so-glamorous clothing range. Can you use your super inflated fox-like intelligence to work out which image should come next in each pattern?

1. **3.**

2. **4.**

Follow that Rat!

Aaaaaaaaaaahhhhhhhh!

My sneaky cousin Mortimer is up to his usual dirty tricks again. This time he has ran off with my supa-styling saucy mousse. Without my special mousse, my prized brush will be just like any other! Help me combat the not-so-glamorous frizz and find Mortimer before this brush is left to seriously flop…

A
B
C
D

FRIZZ

FLOP

FUZZ

Ballroom Basil

Now it's your turn to create your own Basil Brush episode! Check out these photos we've taken from one of our favourite TV episodes, Ballroom Basil. We've left a space underneath each photo for you to write your own script or story. We've put in some speech bubbles for you to add your favourite jokes, too. And remember – anything can happen, there are no rules in showbiz!

Lights, Camera, Reader-ACTION!

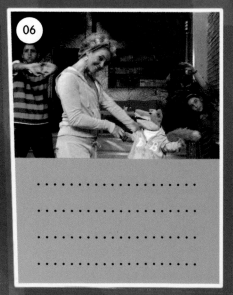

07

08

09

10

11

12

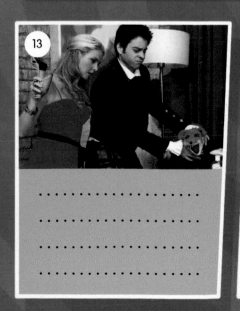

13

14

15

Liam Lancelot

Poor Liam! This photo was taken just after I pelted him with a bow and arrow! He he! Right on the nonce, too! One of the images is slightly different from the others. Can you find the odd one out?

Wacky Wordsearch

I've hidden all of my favourite words in this wordsearch. Can you find them all? The words can read up, down, diagonally and backwards. Good luck!

Showbiz
Television
Party
Friends
Fox
Booming
Boom Boom
Splendiferous
Jelly babies
Spanking
Famous
Fun
Jokes
Brush

```
R T Y U O P B O O L P F A M R Y U S C S
A S E R T R E S R E D C V B N U I M O P
E S P R Y E D T Z I B W O H S R T I H A
S E D L H D C R E T I O P M R C E N L N
D B I E N B P A R T Y T O E S L H I G
S F O N M N N A D R E F O X S N E G J H
X R N O I Y D E R T Y U I O D S V T E N
N I B R M T T I N B S R H N V P I Y L G
J T N R D I T N F A S D E U N A S D L T
L Y N P U N N D Y E N N R I M N I S Y R
P U K I N S O G R L R B T M O K O E B E
I P L S D I H P F E I O N O P I N R A B
U L I R T E S D U N S O U P L N T G B R
Y K S E K O J S N C P M S S I G S J I U
R N J S E R T I L O M B O P N T N K E P
R S O D R I P L N C S O O M H E P L S N
N A K R A S T M N L O O V U S S O P F L
S D R W E R T I O F A M O U S C M C O K
D E F R I E N D S T R E S T O P L I N M
I P O Y T R N H U I L S A W E R T C N H
```

51

Private Den

Ever wish you could just kick back, put your feet up and enjoy a jar of jelly babies or six in peace? Only last week, when I was peacefully indulging in my sugary little delights, I was rudely disturbed by a gaggle of fans. Ahem – ok, ok, it was the cleaner but we can pretend here can't we?! Cut out this do not disturb poster and stick it on your door.

This'll keep them out!

Crossword Caboozle

Shake your mitts and have a go at this randominski crossword! We've chosen a spooky theme in honour of my splendiferous vampire costume! **Good luck!**

ACROSS

01. Often green and sometimes scary
05. Beware if this is full – evil creatures may come to play
07. A witch's favourite mode of transport
09. The frame beneath our skin
10. Ooooooooow! Beware of these howling creatures at night. No place for a handsome fox

DOWN

02. This creepy creature is no problem for a super fox like me!
03. You better grab your stake and garlic
04. You'll see these slabs in a graveyard
06. A vampire's deadly weapon
08. Haunting vision

Don't look behind you – OOOOoo

Basil's Guide to Being Funny in his Most Successful Way

Follow these four (and a half) easy-peasy steps and you will have a trail of fans begging you for more jokes!

✱ STEP ONE
Tell a rip-roaring joke

✱ STEP ONE AND A HALF
Say it like it is the funniest joke you have ever told. Even if it isn't (who said honesty is funny? He he!)

✱ STEP TWO
Pause for two seconds after you have finished your razor sharp joke

✱ STEP THREE
Shout **'Boom! Boom!'** as loud as you can!

✱ STEP FOUR
Burst into raucous, bellowing laughter and don't stop until someone joins in!

Hey, it works for me! Why not use some of the jokes in this book to practise? You never know, this could be the start of a chuckle inducing career!

Pant Alert!

Uh oh! Liam needs our help. He's locked himself out. With just his pants on! And his saucy date, Miss LeBon, is due to arrive in ten minutes. Poor lad. He he! One cannot help but chuckle! Can you help him crack the code and find the key to save him from a life of shame?!

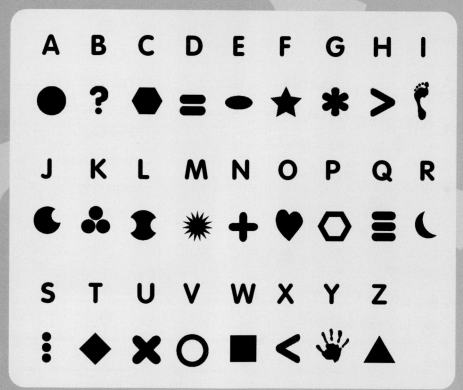

_ _ _ _   _ _ _ _ _   _ _ _   _ _ _

_ _ _ _ _ _ _ _ _ _ _ _ _ _

Fox in Blue

We've just nabbed Mortimer's fake alibi for his whereabouts when he was busy stealing my beloved hairdryer! Let's mix it all up and send it! Imagine his face when he gets a call from the old bill! Priceless. Choose the funniest words from the corresponding bank of words and make it as silly as you can!

Dear PC ~~Harrison~~ .... ● ,

I have a ~~perfect~~ .... ▲ alibi.
At 2pm, at the time of the crime, I was
~~eating~~ .... ◆ in Anil's Café.
I was ~~eating~~ .... ◆ with
my ~~alibi~~ .... ● .

I have a ~~respected~~ ....▲
witness by the name of ~~Dave~~
.... ● . He will tell you
I am a ~~good~~ .... ▲ fox.

Basil Brush is trying to frame a ~~good~~
.... ▲ citizen. In my opinion,
Basil Brush is a ~~terrible~~ .... ★
fox and you should ~~not~~ believe him.

Yours truly,
Mortimer Brush

●
Circle
criminal
waste-of-space
donkey
custard head
bogeyman
vomit face
fool

▲
Triangle
stupid
fake
holey
wonky
ridiculous
suspicious
terrible

◆
Diamond
stealing
fighting
spitting
punching
pick pocketing
robbing
cheating

★
Star
marvellous
trustworthy
respected
wonderful
splendid
delicious
loveable

Hasta La Vista, Foxies!

Now, before the boys in blue catch up with ol' Morty, it's time for us to wish you a booming adieu! The pleasure has been all ours, my trusty Foxes and Foxettes.

So until next time, whether we meet again on the boom box, in a bodacious book, on the theatre stage or if you see me chatting up the ladies on the streets on England – he he! – it can't be too soon. And in the meantime, keep tickling the tonsils of the world with your boom-tastic jokes (just the clean ones though!)

I wish you lots of jelly babies (but hands off the red ones – they're mine!) and the utmost foxiness. Adios!

Basil

Answers

Page 12

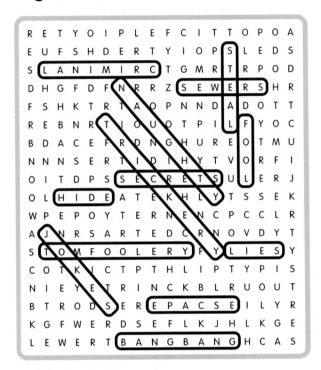

R E T Y O I P L E F C I T T O P O A
E U F S H D E R T Y I O P S L E D S
S L A N I M I R C T G M R T R P O D
D H G F D F N R R Z S E W E R S H R
F S H K T R T A O P N N D A D O T T
R E B N R T I O U O T P I L F Y O C
B D A C E F R D N G H U R E O T M U
N N N S E R T I D I H Y T V O R F I
O I T D P S S E C R E T S U L E R J
O L F H I D E A T E K H L Y T S S E K
W P E P O Y T E R N E N C P C C L R
A J N R S A R T E D C R N O V D Y T
S T O M F O O L E R Y F Y L I E S
C O T K I C T P T H L I P T Y P I S
N I E Y E T R I N C K B L R U O U T
B T R O D S E R E P A C S E I L Y R
K G F W E R D S E F L K J H L K G E
L E W E R T B A N G B A N G H C A S

Page 13

Page 26

1. Crime Botch   5. Bin
2. Dave   6. Madison
3. Red box   7. Boxer shorts
4. Party

Page 27

1. True
2. False
3. True
4. True
5. False
6. False
7. False
8. True

Page 32

1. You don't bury survivors
2. Neither, the frog is dead
3. He was bald
4. Washington DC
5. A hole

Page 36

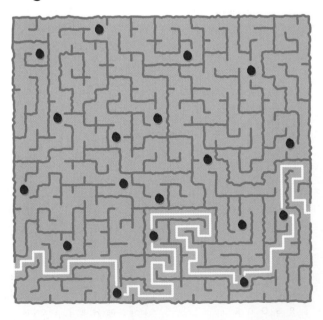

Page 44

Page 46
1. 4
2. 3
3. 2
4. 1

Page 47
1. B

Page 50
1. 03

Page 51

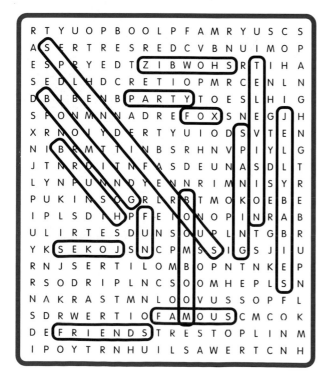

Page 55

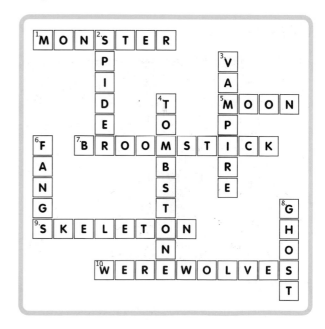

Page 57

THE KEY TO THE DOOR
IS HIDDEN IN ANIL'S TOILET